Original title:
All Despite the Darkness

Copyright © 2024 Book Fairy Publishing
All rights reserved.

Editor: Theodor Taimla
Author: Sandra Squirrel
ISBN HARDBACK: 978-9916-759-16-5
ISBN PAPERBACK: 978-9916-759-17-2

Secrets of a Dim Shine

In the twilight, shadows dance,
Whispers linger in a trance,
Stars above with muted glow,
Guard the secrets we don't know.

Dreams concealed in night's embrace,
Mysteries time cannot erase,
Moonlight's silver, soft and kind,
Holds the tales we'd rather find.

Silent echoes in the breeze,
Carry wonders through the trees,
Glimmers of a past unseen,
Veiled by night's serene sheen.

In the darkness, truths unfold,
Legends of a world untold,
Beneath the skies of somber hue,
Secret stories come to view.

In this realm of soft decline,
Follow paths where stars align,
Dim but shining, clear and near,
Where the hidden does appear.

Beyond the Horizon

Morning breaks with golden light,
Chasing shadows of the night,
Horizons stretch, embrace the day,
Wipe the starlit dreams away.

Journey forth through fields unknown,
Feel the whispers life has sown,
Past the edge where visions blend,
Seek the truths that never end.

Skies above so vast and wide,
Hold the realms we've yet to stride,
Beyond the edge of sight and sound,
Endless worlds are waiting, found.

Let the winds take you afar,
Chase the glimmer of the star,
In the realms where dreams ascend,
Every ending knows no end.

To the distant lines we trace,
Paths unknown, we must embrace,
Beyond the horizon's call,
Find the wonders meant for all.

Silent Sparks

Whispers dance on quiet air,
Night unfolds its secret stare,
Stars alight in velvet dark,
Hearts ignite with silent spark.

Mystic winds through branches weave,
Silent vows in shadows leave,
Moon's embrace, a silver arc,
Dreams awake in silent park.

Soft the glow, a hidden trace,
Echoes fall in fleeting grace,
Timeless realms our souls embark,
Lost in night with silent spark.

Gleaming Through Twilight

Lavender skies in twilight there,
Softest hues the dusk declare,
Whispers gently, shadows play,
Gleaming through the fading day.

Whispers of the dusk arrive,
Breathless moments come alive,
Eyes behold the sky's display,
Gleaming through twilight's bouquet.

Memory and vision blend,
As the day begins to bend,
Stars above, a grand ballet,
Gleaming through an endless sway.

Invisible Gleam

Between the leaves, a hidden light,
Cast by dreams within the night,
Dewdrops catch a whispered beam,
Unseen lights with silent gleam.

Whispers of the stars above,
Faint reflections, tale of love,
Glint in eyes that softly dream,
Worlds beyond an invisible gleam.

Mysteries of night reveal,
Softest truths that daytime seals,
In the dark, a glow supreme,
Guided by an unseen gleam.

Nocturnal Glimmers

Moon imbues the world with grace,
Night reveals its timeless face,
Dreams collide in starry shimmers,
Waltz with quiet nocturnal glimmers.

Soundless beauty, night's embrace,
Stars are pearls in endless space,
Soft the night in gentle whispers,
Bathed in warm nocturnal glimmers.

Twilight fades but spirits rise,
Constellations paint the skies,
Wonders hold, the dawn delivers,
Lingering with nocturnal glimmers.

Veiled Brilliance

In shadows deep where secrets lie,
The silent stars weave vivid dreams,
A tapestry of night's soft sigh,
Where veiled brilliance softly beams.

Mysteries walk the twilight's way,
Whispering winds their tales unfold,
In realms where dusks and dawns replay,
The heart of darkness glows with gold.

Through whispered leaves the moonlight leaves,
A spectral dance of light and shade,
In quiet heartbeats, nature breathes,
With secrets in the night parade.

Moonlight's Embrace

In the quiet of twilight's gleam,
The moon ascends with softest glow,
Enchanting all who dare to dream,
And souls in reverence bow low.

Her silver kiss on troubled waves,
Calms the wildest storm of night,
In moonlight's gentle, soft embrace,
The world finds peace within her light.

Beneath her gaze, the shadows fade,
A tender glow on weary hearts,
In moonlit whispers, night is made,
Where every sorrow soon departs.

Glimmers Through Gloom

Amidst the shadows, faint and dim,
A spark of light begins to rise,
Through shrouded veil and whispered hymn,
Hope's glimmer dances in the skies.

With tender glow, the night inspires,
A beacon bright through darkest shroud,
Illuminating quiet desires,
In dreams expressed both bold and loud.

Through night's embrace, a promise gleams,
In every heart it plants a seed,
Glimmers through gloom, in starlit streams,
Of courage, love, and gentle deed.

Hidden Radiance

In every heart a flame concealed,
A hidden radiance burns bright,
Behind the veils of sorrows healed,
Awakens dreams in silent night.

Beneath the stars' celestial sheen,
A quiet strength in shadows thrived,
In darkness rich with silver keen,
The essence of the night survived.

A glow within, unseen by day,
Emerges in the twilight's glow,
In hidden radiance, night's array,
A secret light few come to know.

The Glow Within

In the silence of the night,
A hidden ember gleams,
Whispers of a distant light,
Awakening lost dreams.

Deep within a heart confined,
A spark begins to rise,
With every beat, a flame designed,
To warm the darkest skies.

Secrets in the shadows kept,
Now softly start to shine,
In hollows where the sorrow slept,
A beacon's bold design.

Embrace the glow that grows inside,
Let doubts and fears rescind,
And in the light you've long denied,
Find courage to transcend.

Lights Through the Black

Underneath the starlit canopy,
Beyond the edge of sight,
A thousand flames of memory,
Illuminate the night.

Guiding paths through midnight shade,
Their glow a tender mark,
To brave the unknown unafraid,
A lantern in the dark.

In every shimmer, stories cast,
From ages lost in time,
Their whispers from the farthest past,
Resonate through rhyme.

Together we will chase the hue,
That breaks the sable mold,
And find a universe anew,
In spilled celestial gold.

Unseen Radiance

A hidden light beyond the veil,
Invisible yet clear,
Its brilliance in the shadows trail,
For those who dare draw near.

In every soul, a secret flame,
Unseen but ever warm,
Its whisper is a sacred name,
Amidst the gathering storm.

A guiding star within us all,
It beckons soft and bright,
To rise above where shadows fall,
And claim our inner light.

Let not the dim of night deceive,
The sparks that blaze ahead,
For radiance is ours to weave,
Though silent words are said.

Tenacity in Twilight

As day gives way to tender dusk,
And shadows softly creep,
A strength within begins to musk,
The fears that make us weep.

In twilight's hold, a courage gleams,
A hope that's bound with steel,
Emerging from fragmented dreams,
With power to reveal.

Defying darkness that encroaches,
We rise with steady might,
Resilient as the dawn approaches,
A beacon in the night.

Through twilight's trials we ascend,
With fervor and with grace,
In every heart, a light to tend,
To challenge and embrace.

Through Veil of Midnight

In silence creeps the sable night,
Veils of shadow, absence of light.
Whispers weave through ancient trees,
Secrets carried by the breeze.

Moonlight threads through inky shrouds,
Weaving lace among the clouds.
Stars ignite in distant arcs,
Guiding hearts through darkened parks.

Midnight's veil, a mystic cloak,
Dreams awaken as we invoke.
Wanderers seek solace there,
In the night's enshrouded care.

Silent Luminescence

Underneath the still of dawn,
Light emerges, shadows drawn.
Silent glow on dewy leaves,
Morning's gentle web it weaves.

Whispers soft as night departs,
Embers warm the day's first hearts.
Radiance builds, softly hums,
Daylight's hymn in twilight's drums.

Gone the stars, the sun ascends,
Through the quiet light extends.
An ethereal dance without sound,
Luminescence all around.

Stars Beneath Eclipses

In shadow's dance the stars reveal,
Hidden worlds they slowly peel.
Beneath the moon's eclipsing kiss,
Mysteries found in astral bliss.

Galaxies in dark embrace,
Hold a shimmer, hold a trace.
Light and dark in cosmic waltz,
Heavenly beauty, no faults.

Ephemeral moments in night's grasp,
Starry secrets, softly clasp.
Witness dreams in silent flight,
Stars beneath eclipses' night.

Embers in the Abyss

Down in darkness, embers glow,
Where the depths of shadows grow.
Fire's heart in cavern's gloom,
Flickers fiercely through the room.

Ancient stones hold memories,
Silent whispers, histories.
Light emerges, then it fades,
Mystic warmth the deep persuades.

Embers dance in voids so vast,
Echoes of a timeless past.
In the abyss, find solace there,
Flames of hope against despair.

The Hidden Glow

Beneath the earth, the embers sleep,
A silent fire, so warm and deep.
The shadows cloak its gentle light,
A hidden glow beneath the night.

Whispers soft, the flames arise,
Reflecting stars within the skies.
Though buried deep, its aura shows,
In dreams, the hidden glow bestows.

In hearts untouched by cold despair,
The hidden glow is always there.
Eternal warmth, it softly sows,
In kindred souls, the ember grows.

Glints of Distant Hope

Across the void, the stars align,
With silent whispers, they do shine.
In darkness deep, a spark is lit,
Glints of hope, they softly flit.

Beyond the reach of weary sighs,
The glints of hope in darkened skies.
Guiding hearts with gentle fire,
Each spark a beacon of desire.

Through the haze of doubt and fear,
Distant glints of hope appear.
Embrace the light, let courage grow,
In night's embrace, the glimmers show.

Luminous Defiance

In the shadow of despair,
A light burned bright, a rebel's flare.
Against the night and all its chains,
Luminous defiance reigns.

Through the storms and vengeful skies,
A beacon fierce, unwavering, flies.
To every heart, it boldly brings,
The courage of unbroken wings.

Stand defiant, let light pour,
From every wound and every pore.
In the dark, it dares to fight,
Defiance glowing, pure and bright.

Eclipsed by Brilliance

The night would claim the world again,
Yet brilliance dared to mark its pen.
In shadows deep, a light persists,
Eclipsed but never quite dismissed.

A stellar clash of dark and light,
In heaven's dome, an ageless fight.
From the void, the stars emerge,
New brilliance on the edge's verge.

Though eclipsed, it still does gleam,
In every heart, a radiant dream.
Through darkest times, we find our stance,
Eclipsed, but always given chance.

Pulses of Light

In the shadows deep, a glow starts to rise,
Through the murk, a beacon in disguise.
Stars align to form a radiant chain,
Pulses of light, dispelling the pain.

Whispers in the dark, the silence breaks,
Guiding us forward, each step it takes.
Mystery unfurls, truth in sight,
Charting our course with pulses of light.

In the heart of night, we find our grace,
Echoes of luminescence in each space.
Hopes are woven into the bright,
Lives enriched in pulses of light.

Flickers of Tenacity

In the midst of chaos, a flame ignites,
Flickers of tenacity in the night.
Through the storm, we silently fight,
Holding on to bits of flickering light.

Strength summoned in the smallest spark,
A glow becomes fierce, dispelling the dark.
Unyielding courage takes its flight,
With every flicker of tenacious light.

Through each trial, our spirits endure,
Resilience captured in light so pure.
The journey's hard, but hearts burn bright,
Driven by flickers of tenacity, our light.

Invisible Illumination

Quiet whispers of light in the unseen,
Illuminating paths where darkness had been.
Guiding silently, a steadfast sentinel,
Invisible illumination, so gentle.

In the silence, our spirits ignite,
Finding solace in the softest light.
Through veils of darkness, hope gleams,
Invisible threads stitching our dreams.

Woven through the night, a silent guide,
Encouraging us, lighting what's inside.
With every step, illumination grows,
Invisible yet bright, our journey shows.

Through the Cloak

Beneath the cloak of the darkest night,
A hidden glow begins its flight.
Soft and subtle, yet gathering grace,
Piercing through the cloak, a light we embrace.

Unseen forces shape our way,
Guiding our footsteps, keeping fears at bay.
Through shadows dense, we find our scope,
With light emerging through the cloak of hope.

In mysteries deep, truths are revealed,
By a light that's pure and unconcealed.
Through every trial and distant yoke,
Our hearts are warmed as we pierce the cloak.

Light

In the quiet dawn, a sliver of gold,
Stories of light begin to unfold.
Through the day, it dances and weaves,
Casting warmth on all it believes.

Beacons in darkness, a promise kept,
Guiding those who roam and who've wept.
In every shadow, it finds its place,
Light, eternal, in time and space.

Moments of joy and battles won,
Illuminated by the enduring sun.
A radiant force, pure and bright,
In endless forms, we cherish the light.

Whispers in the Gloom

In the stillness of the night,
Stars weave tales with their light,
Echoes of ancient rune,
Whispers in the gloom.

Veils of shadows softly dance,
Beneath the moon's silver lance,
Secrets kept in twilight's bloom,
Whispers in the gloom.

Through the forest, breezes flow,
Carrying whispers, soft and low,
Leaves rustle in a mystical loom,
Whispers in the gloom.

Beneath the blanket of the skies,
The truth in shadows lies,
Murmurs in the midnight room,
Whispers in the gloom.

As the dawn begins to loom,
Dispelling whispers in the gloom,
Night retreats, day's gentle broom,
Whispers in the gloom.

Light's Silent Victory

Through the valleys dark and still,
Light's tender rays fulfill,
Every shadow's silent plea,
Light's silent victory.

Morning breaks with gentle fire,
Banishing night's dark attire,
With each ray, a symphony,
Light's silent victory.

In the quiet of the dawn,
Softly, darkness is withdrawn,
Day emerges, proud and free,
Light's silent victory.

Through the windows, warm and bright,
Shines the promise of the light,
Echoes of eternity,
Light's silent victory.

Each new day a silent cheer,
Conquering the night's deep fear,
Hope restored so vividly,
Light's silent victory.

Courage Beyond Shadows

In the heart of deepest night,
Courage finds its will to fight,
Against the darkest shadow's might,
Courage beyond shadows.

Through the trials of the unseen,
Strength arises sharp and keen,
Shining through the darkened meadows,
Courage beyond shadows.

When the world's a storm of fear,
Steadfast hearts will persevere,
Guiding light through darkened hallows,
Courage beyond shadows.

No defeat can quell the brave,
Nor could despair make them cave,
They find hope where terror swallows,
Courage beyond shadows.

At the dawn of each new day,
Fear's illusions swept away,
In the light that always follows,
Courage beyond shadows.

Radiance Against the Night

Stars ignite the velvet black,
Guiding lost souls on their track,
Ancient beacons burning bright,
Radiance against the night.

Moonbeams kiss the quiet earth,
In their glow, a quiet birth,
Of dreams and hopes taking flight,
Radiance against the night.

Through the darkness, bold and true,
Light pierces the heavy blue,
Bringing vision, sweet delight,
Radiance against the night.

In each heart, a shining spark,
Chasing shadows, banishing dark,
With a strength, an inner light,
Radiance against the night.

As the sun prepares to rise,
Painting colors in the skies,
Day replaces, pure and white,
Radiance against the night.

Eternal Beacons

In the sky, so vast and grand,
Stars like ancient spirits stand,
Guiding sailors 'cross the sea,
Marking time's eternity.

In the stillness of the night,
Whispers borne by soft moonlight,
Legends told and dreams unfurled,
Echoes through this endless world.

Light that travels eons far,
From a long-forgotten star,
Illuminates our fleeting days,
With its everlasting rays.

Transient Shimmers

Moments caught in twilight's grace,
Fleeting glimmers in life's race,
Ephemeral and soft they glow,
Like the gentle falling snow.

Kisses of the morning sun,
Disappear when day is done,
Memories of warmth and light,
Fade into the coming night.

In the dusk they softly gleam,
Echoes of a distant dream,
Shadows dance and spirits rise,
Fading into star-kissed skies.

Emerging Brilliance

From the dark, a spark ignites,
Banishing the endless nights,
Hope takes form in gentle rays,
Turning gloom to brighter days.

From the quiet of the morn,
Brilliance new and freshly born,
Rises with the dawn's first light,
Breaking free from deepest night.

In each soul a flame resides,
Guiding through life's winds and tides,
Brilliance destined to emerge,
In a radiant, timeless surge.

We Shine

In the face of darkest night,
Together we ignite the light,
Hand in hand and heart to heart,
We create a brilliance start.

Through the trials, through the storm,
In our strength, our spirits warm,
Bound by courage, love, and hope,
Together, always, we will cope.

We shine bright, the world to see,
Together, strong and ever free,
Against the dark, our light will stand,
United in this radiant band.

Sparks of Survival

In the heart of darkness, embers fly,
Glowing against the raven sky.
Fires of hope in the cold wind sigh,
Whispering 'fear not, for you can try.'

The world turns bleak, shadows creep,
Yet spirits rise, no thoughts of sleep.
Through the veil of night, dreams seep,
Igniting flames that ever keep.

Among the ruins, hearts ignite,
Fragile yet fierce, burning bright.
Through tempest winds, they take their flight,
Guided by that eternal light.

Though storms may shake and mountains fall,
Within the spirit's endless hall,
Resilience thrives within us all,
As sparks of survival heed the call.

Through shattered glass and broken stone,
Courage seeds where fear has grown.
In every ember, light is sown,
Forged by the battles we've known.

The Hushed Glow

In quiet moments, silence speaks,
Softly weaving through the weeks.
A golden hue in twilight peaks,
Revealing truths the heart seeks.

Whispered winds, a gentle breeze,
Rustle leaves with graceful ease.
The world in shadows, none to tease,
Finds its solace in night's release.

Stars above in silent choir,
Kindle dreams and hearts' desire.
An ephemeral, hushed fire,
Setting spirits ever higher.

Each soft glimmer, each dim light,
Carries stories through the night.
Ephemeral beams, pure and bright,
Offer comfort in their flight.

In this hush, a glow profound,
Echoes peace without a sound.
Through the stillness, dreams are found,
In the night's embrace, unbound.

Veins of Radiance

Golden rivers through the sky,
Veins of radiance running high.
Streaks of dawn as night bids bye,
A canvas where the dreams lie.

Through the clouds, the sunlight weaves,
A tapestry as day conceives.
Glistening threads of morning eves,
Embroidering what heart believes.

Earth awakens, whispers flow,
In the fields where wildflowers grow.
Every petal starts to glow,
With secrets only nature knows.

Azure heavens, endless blue,
Cradle life in each new hue.
Sunbeams dance where shadows flew,
Painting worlds in light's debut.

From the depths of night and shade,
Resplendent rays of day invade.
In every curve and line displayed,
Veins of radiance serenade.

Twilight Resiliency

As the sun dips low, sky aglow,
Twilight softens all we know.
Between the night and day's tableau,
Resilient hearts begin to show.

In the dusk, a strength revealed,
In colors that the day concealed.
With every twilight's shade appealed,
Layers of courage are unsealed.

Shadows stretch and light transforms,
Silent vows in muted forms.
Through the calm before the storms,
Faith withstands, and hope conforms.

In this twilight, quiet might,
Souls take flight in fading light.
Wounds of day heal in the night,
Resilient through the darkest plight.

From sunrise dreams, to twilight's grace,
In every hue and every space,
Resiliency finds its place,
In the ever-changing face.

The Glint Beyond

In twilight's tender grasp, a world unfolds,
Where shadows weave, and secrets gently told.
Stars etch their tales across the velvet skies,
A glint beyond, as endless as our sighs.

The moon, a lantern in the midnight sea,
Guides wayfarers to dreams, where spirits flee.
Through whispered winds and whispers of the past,
We chase the flicker, faint but ever last.

Oceans of night, in silence they concede,
To journeys born of twilight's whispered creed.
In every shadow, hope's bright ember burns,
The glint beyond, to which our heart returns.

Dusk's Eternal Ember

When day retires to its golden bed,
And dusk unfurls its cloak of crimson red,
The sky ignites with whispers, soft and low,
As embered hues in twilight set aglow.

The world in hush, a canvas of the night,
Paints dreams in shades of tender amber light.
Each star, a fleck of eternity's fire,
Burns brightly in the heavens' open choir.

A tranquil moment, poised in silent grace,
Where time once stopped, a resting dreamer's face.
Dusk holds the secrets of tomorrow's gaze,
An ember's glow within the night's embrace.

Nightfall's Glint

The sky descends with whispers dark and deep,
As night awakens from its crimson sleep.
Soft glints of silver dance on velvet waves,
Nightfall's kiss, in twilight's gentle caves.

A mystery that twinkles in the sky,
With every star, a question burning high.
The world in stillness, shadows gently sway,
Nightfall's glint guides wanderers on their way.

In every leaf, a sigh of evening's tune,
And dreams ignited neath the tender moon.
We find our solace in this glimmered light,
In nightfall's glint, our hearts take flight.

Shimmering Solitude

When silence falls, and whispers of the day,
Dissolve in night's serene and quiet play.
A shimmering solitude of peace unfolds,
Where stars like stories, in the ether, told.

The moon's embrace, a lover's gentle hand,
Guides solitudes across a dreaming land.
Through vast expanse, where heartbeats softly tread,
In shimmering tides of night, our thoughts are led.

Each breath we take, a chapter in the night,
Unveiling depths of luminescent light.
In tranquil corners of the soul's domain,
Shimmering solitude, our hearts retain.

Glimpses from the Deep

Beneath the waves of azure blue,
Lies a world of silence, calm but true.
In shadows dark, and corals bright,
Creatures dance in the soft moonlight.

Whispers of currents, stories in flow,
Secrets of the deep, none yet know.
A shimmer of scales, flash and flirt,
In the cool embrace of the ocean's skrt.

Mysteries unfold in the coral bowers,
Unseen realms, like hidden flowers.
Ancient whispers, tales untold,
In the sea's embrace, mysteries old.

Glimpses of wonders, hidden below,
Silent symphony's graceful show.
Bubbles rise, dreams take flight,
In the deep's comforting night.

Echoes from realms untouched by light,
Cosmic dance in the still of night.
Ocean's breath, in gentle sweep,
Glimpses from the deep, secrets they keep.

Ray Through the Pitch

In darkness dense, a solitary gleam,
Pierces through like a whispered dream.
A beacon's glow, in the vast unknown,
Guides each step, though not alone.

Night's embrace with arms so wide,
Cloaks the path where shadows hide.
Yet through the pitch, a ray shines true,
Lighting hearts with vibrant hue.

Hope ignites in spectral flow,
With each flicker, shadows go.
Through despair, a guiding light,
Parting dark, revealing sight.

A single beam, courage lends,
In the night, where story bends.
By its glow, fates entwine,
In the darkness, stars align.

Ray through the pitch, steadfast and bright,
Bringing dawn to the endless night.
In its glow, faith is reborn,
Lighting paths till the break of morn.

Guiding Glimmers

Tiny sparks in the twilight's grace,
Guiding stars in the vast embrace.
In their light, dreams take flight,
Comforting hearts in the silent night.

Through life's maze, a gentle glow,
Marking paths where we should go.
In their warmth, fears dissolve,
Guiding glimmers, mysteries solve.

Each small light, a tale to tell,
Of courage found where shadows dwell.
In their dance, hope renews,
Dreams alight where darkness hues.

By their side, we walk the night,
Seeking truths in soft starlight.
In their glow, spirits rise,
Guided by the night's wise eyes.

Guiding glimmers in the silent dark,
A celestial map, our course to mark.
With each step, under their watchful beam,
Journey onwards, through starry dream.

Spark in the Void

In the vast expanse, where silence reigns,
A tiny spark, the dark disdains.
From the void, a light anew,
Whispers softly, dreams pursue.

Life's enigma in the endless sway,
Spark ignites the night to day.
Illuminates the shadow's art,
Brings to life the hidden part.

In emptiness, a flicker pure,
Gives to darkness, a silent cure.
Guides the weary, lost in night,
With its tender, steadfast light.

Hope resides within its glow,
In the void, where dreams flow.
A beacon strong, against the dark,
In its warmth, fears embark.

Spark in the void, eternal and bright,
Casting hope by gentle light.
In vastness deep, its promise shown,
Bringing the lost ones safely home.

Beacon of Dusk

As the sun begins its slow descent,
Colors of amber paint the skies,
A tranquil hush envelopes the land,
Where silence and serenity lies.

Caressed by twilight's gentle hand,
Shadows gracefully extend,
A beacon of dusk embraces all,
Bringing daytime to an end.

The meadow whispers soft goodbyes,
To the fading warmth of light,
Nature's lullaby gently sways,
Welcoming the tender night.

Stars ignite their distant glow,
In the canvas of the dark,
Imbuing dreams with twinkling hope,
A night song's sweet remark.

Thus, the beacon of dusk proclaims,
An end ensconced in peace,
With promises of morning rays,
When night's silence will cease.

Light Over the Night

Beneath the canopy of stars,
A silver moon ascends high,
Casting light over the night,
Illuminating the sky.

Silent whispers of the breeze,
Dance through the midnight air,
Echoing the gentle waves,
Calm reflections everywhere.

Oceans shimmer under moon,
With tides in rhythmic dance,
Nature's ballet performed each night,
In a timeless, sweet romance.

Mountains stand like sentinels,
Guardians of the nocturne,
Where shadows merge with twilight hues,
And ember fires still burn.

Thus the light over the night,
Guides us through the dark unknown,
A celestial glow of hope,
Until the dawn is shown.

Witness the Glisten

In the silent hush of midnight,
Moonlight bathes the sleeping earth,
Silver threads weave through the night,
Birth of dreams' gentle mirth.

Crystals on the dewy leaves,
Catch the sparkle of the sky,
Witness the glisten soft and bright,
As time quietly glides by.

Stars above, like diamond tears,
Adorn the velvet dome,
Light's embrace to shadows dear,
A celestial, tender poem.

Rivers gleam with liquid light,
Mirroring the heavens' sheen,
Nature's treasures hidden in night,
In magic's serene scene.

Let the dreams of night unfold,
Beneath the starry, gleaming reign,
Witness the glisten, timeless told,
Until dawn returns again.

After the Dusk

When the sun dips low to rest,
And dusk envelopes the earth,
Night awakens in its splendor,
In shadows, dreams find birth.

After the dusk, the stars appear,
Guardians of the silent night,
Whispers of the cosmos near,
In darkness gleaming bright.

The calm of night spreads like a veil,
Over land and sleepy sea,
Mysteries in silence dwell,
Where night's secrets wander free.

Owls whisper their nocturnal song,
Beneath the moon's soft gaze,
In the quiet, time moves along,
Marking hours in a daze.

Thus after dusk, the night commands,
With peaceful, soothing spell,
Drawing dreams with gentle hands,
Till dawn breaks night's farewell.

Twilight's Glow

As the sun dips low in the sky,
Colors of dusk start to unfurl,
Whispers of night begin to fly,
Painting dreams upon the world.

Soft hues of orange and pink blend,
With the deep azure of the night,
Stars emerging, message they send,
Twilight's glow, oh what a sight.

Shadows dance upon the ground,
Nature's lullaby starts to play,
In the twilight's gentle surround,
Daylight slowly fades away.

A cool breeze carries secrets,
Of the day that's come to rest,
In the stillness of the sunset,
Hearts find peace, they are blessed.

Silence settles, calm and sweet,
Nighttime's embrace, a tender hold,
Twilight's glow, a path we meet,
Into dreams both brave and bold.

The Subtle Blaze

A flicker in the dark, unseen,
A fire burns with quiet might,
Its warmth and strength it does convene,
In shadows hidden from the light.

Embers glow with steady pride,
Whispering tales of days now past,
The flames they rise, then coincide,
With dreams that in our souls are cast.

The subtle blaze, a guiding spark,
Through tempest winds and stormy seas,
A beacon in the night so dark,
That calls forth courage with such ease.

In every heart there lies a flame,
A source of life's unyielding will,
And though it might not wear a name,
Its presence you can always feel.

So nurture well the fire within,
Let it burn both fierce and slow,
For in its glow true strength begins,
In the subtle blaze we grow.

Against the Abyss

In shadows deep where fears reside,
A soul stands firm, a beacon bright,
With courage as its trusted guide,
It fights against the endless night.

The abyss calls with haunting cries,
Whispers of doubt and dread it sows,
But steadfast are the daring eyes,
That face the dark, their strength it knows.

Each step is taken with resolve,
Towards the precipice so vast,
For in this journey, one evolves,
And finds the strength to hold steadfast.

Though shadows loom and threaten near,
The heart beats with a fierce intent,
To conquer every lurking fear,
With hope and will, it won't relent.

Against the abyss, one must fight,
With every breath and heart's desire,
For in the darkest, coldest night,
The soul's true strength will then inspire.

Moon's Rebel Light

Under the veil of night's embrace,
A silver glow begins its rise,
The moon with defiant grace,
Illumines the darkened skies.

Her light defies the weight of night,
Casting shadows that dance wild,
In her presence, all seems right,
Mysteries of the dark beguiled.

Rebel beams illuminate the earth,
Touching hearts and stirring dreams,
The moon's glow, a symbol of rebirth,
In her light, our spirit gleams.

Against the dark, she strides alone,
A beacon of hope, pure and bright,
Her luminescence, fiercely known,
A guardian through the night.

So let the moon's rebellion guide,
Through shadows thick and paths uncharted,
In her light, we shall confide,
With every night, anew, we're started.

Midnight Embers

In the quiet, stars ignite,
Whispers merge with soft moonlight.
Embers glow in darkened skies,
Dreams take flight, shadows rise.

Eternal dance of timeless space,
Hearts by flame, a gentle trace.
Mystic echoes softly sway,
Guided through the night's ballet.

Twilight's breath, a tender breeze,
Stirs the dark with ancient ease.
Flicker, flicker, sparks so bright,
Guardians of the silent night.

Steadfast Luminescence

Through the veil of twilight's brim,
Pierces light, though edges dim.
Steadfast beams a path unfold,
Guided by a heart that's bold.

Stars may shift, the night be long,
But the light remains so strong.
Chasing shadows, holding fast,
Through the night 'til dawn at last.

In the dark, persist with grace,
Glistening in each secret place.
Luminous in steadfast fight,
Illuminates the boundless night.

Lustrous Nightfall

Whispers in the evening's glow,
Moonlit paths where dreams may flow.
Nightfall brings a silent peace,
Restful breaths and hearts at ease.

Starlit realms where wishes spark,
Guided through the velvet dark.
Every shimmer holds a prayer,
Softly cast upon the air.

Deep within the midnight's thrall,
Lies the magic of nightfall.
Twinkling lights, a gentle call,
Celestial whispers to us all.

After the Shadow

After shadows drift away,
Comes the promise of the day.
Hope reborn in morning glow,
Guidance in the light we know.

Worries fade as dawn proceeds,
Light now sows its cosmic seeds.
In the hues of breaking dawn,
New day's breath brings sweet respawn.

Life emerges from the shade,
Sunlight weaves through night's parade.
Renewal in each golden ray,
Banishing the dark away.

Shine

In the darkness, find your gleam,
Brightest star within your dream.
Even when the night is deep,
Light remains, a promise keep.

Radiance within your soul,
Guides you toward a brighter goal.
Shimmer, glitter, ever pure,
Through the night, you can endure.

In your heart, the light will shine,
Softly through each shadowed line.
Beacon in the darkest times,
Guiding stars, celestial chimes.

Threads of Silver

In twilight's gentle, waning hour,
Threads of silver weave their art.
Casting a glistening, woven bower,
Binding heaven, earth, and heart.

Moonbeams filter through the canopy,
A gossamer web of night divine.
Caught between the leaves' sweet fantasy,
Where dreams and reality entwine.

The night, a seamstress with deft hands,
Stitches the world in soft embrace.
Whispering tales through quiet lands,
Each silver thread a delicate trace.

Stars align in silent vow,
Glistening with soft, ethereal grace.
In the night's gentle, calming brow,
We find serenity's hidden place.

Threads of silver, faint but strong,
Guide us through the shadowed deep.
In the weaver's ancient, whispered song,
We find our dreams and secrets keep.

Depth's Beacon

In the cavern dark and vast,
A light appears, a beaming spark.
Guiding souls that wander past,
Through shadows deep, both near and stark.

In silence, through the shadows cast,
The beacon whispers, soft and kind.
An anchor for the souls amassed,
Lost in dreams, in thoughts confined.

A flicker brave, against the night,
It calls us to a distant shore.
A guide that sparks our inner light,
And casts our fears forevermore.

Hope's bright shimmer, gently creeping,
Through the crevices of doubt.
In its glow, we find a keeping,
A path that leads us out.

Depth's beacon, steadfast, never fading,
Illuminates the dark unknown.
In its glow, our fears abating,
A guiding star, forever shown.

Chasing the Faint Flame

Through the dusk where shadows play,
A faint flame dances, calls my name.
O'er hills where twilight meets the day,
I wander forth, in search of flame.

The flicker's warmth, a fleeting trace,
In the night's embrace, it leads the way.
Guiding through the wild unknown space,
Where dreams and memories sway.

A lantern in the velveteen,
It wavers, but it never fades.
A promise of what might have been,
And all the magic it invades.

Through forest whispers, hush and still,
I chase the light, so wild and free.
Into the night, up yonder hill,
To where the flame is meant to be.

Chasing dreams, we journey far,
Through heart's deep woods and past the gave.
For the faint flame is our guiding star,
A light that dares us to be brave.

Resilient Glow

Amid the storm's relentless howl,
A resilient glow dares to persist.
Amidst the dark, where shadows prowl,
Its ember sings, with silent twist.

Through trials fierce and battles fought,
The glow endures, unwavering bright.
Kindling hope in hearts distraught,
A beacon in the darkest night.

Strength is found in gentle whispers,
In the quiet glow's embrace.
Against the night, with light that lingers,
A testament of endless grace.

In the silence, fierce and deep,
The glow ignites our soul's resolve.
A promise to the veins that weep,
That in its light, we all evolve.

Resilient glow, forever burning,
Through the darkest night and woe.
A flame within, always yearning,
For brighter days, where dreams flow.

The Night's Rebellion

In the shadow's grasp, the stars convene,
Whispers of tales that might have been.
Silent winds begin to sigh,
Rebellion rumbles in the sky.

Moonlight dances on the crest,
Of waves that never find their rest.
Cloaked in veils of midnight's hue,
Whispers of defiance grew.

Through the forest, shadows creep,
Awakening those who dare to sleep.
Amid the branches' muffled screams,
A rise of long-forgotten dreams.

Piercing through, an astronomy,
Constellations break free.
Nebulas of a nebulous night,
Revolt against the dying light.

In the morning's quiet fall,
Echoes of the night's enthrall.
An uprising under cryptic skies,
A realm where rebel spirits rise.

Light in the Hidden Corners

Beneath the ancient timber's arch,
Glow settled in the autumn march.
A glimmering through the shaded path,
As shadows play in silent wrath.

Between the rocks and crumbled stone,
Where daylight seems a world unknown.
A soft, persistent glow does fight,
Bringing hidden truths to light.

A flicker near the broken gate,
Past memories that resonate.
From deep within the haunted halls,
A luminance that never stalls.

Find courage in the darkened twist,
A spark where doubt and fear exist.
For even in the dimmest nooks,
The smallest light reveals new looks.

Journeys marked by subtle gleams,
Follow hope within your dreams.
In every shadowed, silent place,
Light meets dark, face to face.

Beneath Darkened Skies

Silent echos fill the night,
Beneath the skies devoid of light.
Dreams and fears intertwine,
Under constellations, signs align.

Whispering winds through canopies,
Brush against the forest's pleas.
Every rustle, its own tune,
In the shadow of the moon.

Shadows stretch across the plain,
Mirroring an endless chain.
Within the silence, secrets lie,
Masked beneath the darkened sky.

Ancient tales that once were told,
In the night's embrace unfold.
Mysteries within the night,
Silent screams devoid of fright.

Stars pierced through the inky veil,
Shining truths that never fail.
In realms where dark and light reprise,
Journeys start 'neath darkened skies.

Hints of Dawn

As night fades to pastel skies,
The morning whispers slow goodbyes.
Faint hints of dawn, the day's embrace,
Emerging from its shadowed place.

Soft hues of pink and amber gold,
The secrets of the night unfold.
Beneath the canopy of dreams,
Awakening to morning's gleam.

The horizon hums a gentle hue,
Where dreams are born anew.
Stars retreat to hide away,
As dawn prepares the coming day.

In the quiet of the early light,
Courage takes its flight.
A promise in the new day's rise,
Where hope and glory kiss the skies.

Moments caught between the lines,
Of night and day, where light defines.
Whispers of a world reborn,
In the sacred hints of dawn.

Beyond the Murk

In shadows deep, where whispers sway,
Murk enshrouds the light of day.
Through veils of dusk and clouded haze,
Hope emerges, bright sun's rays.

Silent echoes, secrets told,
Beneath the moon, in silver fold.
Darkness wanes as dawn breaks through,
A promise kept, a sky of blue.

Horizon gleams, the night retreats,
Twilight's grasp meets soft defeat.
In the heart of every shadow's bloom,
Lies the birth of morning's plume.

Stars may fade, their light concealed,
Yet dreams in murk remain revealed.
Through the silent, velvet black,
Emerge the paths we thought we'd lack.

The Bright Shadow

Beneath the eye of twilight's tears,
A bright shadow hides, draws near.
Softly glowing, whispers light,
Promises of stars in night.

In fields where silence blooms and sways,
Shadows dance in twilight's gaze.
Glimmers hint where light conceals,
Secrets told the night reveals.

Echoes sing in sabled hues,
Midnight breathes its gentle clues.
Whispers blend with dreams that gleam,
Silent soul, a shadow's beam.

Golden gleam in deepened shade,
Moonlit paths by stars conveyed.
Through the black, a beacon found,
In shadows bright, our hopes are bound.

Dusklit Glimmers

When the sun dips low, skies embrace,
Dusklit glimmers warm the space.
Stars begin their secret flight,
Guiding dreams through soft twilight.

Whispers of the day's embrace,
Yield to night in gentle trace.
Hues of amber, shades of gold,
Craft the stories darkness told.

Lanterns flicker, shadows dance,
In the twilight's soft expanse.
Curtains drawn by evening's hand,
Reveal the stars, a night-time band.

Quiet streams and evening's breeze,
Carry whispers through the trees.
Dusklit glimmers, pathway bright,
Leads us through the gentle night.

Midnight's Promise

Underneath the sable sky,
Midnight's promise whispers by.
Stars like lanterns light the way,
Night's embrace until the day.

Veiled in silver, shadows gleam,
Midnight's lake, a mirrored dream.
Softly tread the paths of night,
Where the moon's soft glow is bright.

Silent vows in darkness keep,
As the world begins to sleep.
Breathing life through whispered glow,
Nighttime's chapters, secrets show.

Deep within the quiet's hold,
Promises of dreams unfold.
Every star a silent pledge,
Midnight's promise, on the edge.

Stars Beneath the Clouds

In shadows deep and skies so grey,
Beneath the world where dreams do play,
The stars ignite with softest glow,
A secret light the heart will know.

Through mist and fog, their whispers creep,
A silent song that heavens keep,
Guiding souls with hidden beams,
In twilight's touch and moonlit dreams.

Beyond the veil of night's embrace,
They shimmer in their sacred space,
Lost to sight but felt so clear,
A cosmic dance that draws us near.

Beneath the clouds, in realms unseen,
They twinkle with a light serene,
A compass through the darkest night,
These stars that shine without our sight.

Silent guides in shadowed skies,
They lead us where our spirit flies,
And though the world may dim and shroud,
We find our way by stars beneath the clouds.

Undying Light

In the heart of endless night,
Lies a flame forever bright,
A beacon through the stormy seas,
A light that whispers hope with ease.

When darkness falls and shadows grow,
This undying light will always glow,
Through trials vast and paths unknown,
Its warmth and courage gently shown.

No tempest wild nor fearsome gale,
Can dim this light or make it pale,
It stands against the tide of fate,
A steadfast flame to illuminate.

With every dawn and twilight's hand,
It touches lives across the land,
An ancient strength that fuels the soul,
In every heart it makes us whole.

So trust this light when night is long,
It builds the weak, it makes us strong,
An endless fire that never dies,
Guiding stars in our human skies.

Illuminated Shadows

In the corners where shadows dance,
Lies a light that takes a chance,
It penetrates the darkest nooks,
Illuminates what fear forsook.

Within the depth where secrets hide,
A gentle glow does softly bide,
Revealing truths in muted hues,
A light the shadow can't refuse.

It paints the dark with silken beams,
Weaving through forgotten dreams,
Unveiling stories held in night,
A silent muse of hidden light.

The shadows yield and form anew,
Underneath this radiant view,
A balance struck in chiaroscuro,
Between the dark and light's bravura.

So let the shadows freely fall,
For in their midst, the light stands tall,
An artful blend of dark and bright,
Creating beauty in the fight.

Hope in the Abyss

Beneath the depths where darkness reigns,
An ember glows through silent pains,
A spark of hope that dares to be,
A light within the blackened sea.

In caverns cold and void profound,
This gleam of faith is often found,
It whispers through the silent chill,
A promise that persists with will.

Through endless night and shadows thick,
This hope emerges, ever slick,
It dances with the unseen rays,
A beacon through the foggy haze.

When all seems lost in void's embrace,
It holds a light within its grace,
Guiding souls in their despair,
A timeless hope beyond compare.

So in the abyss, do not fear,
For hope is always drawing near,
A flame that never dies nor fades,
A light that pierces through the shades.

Lonely Starlight

In the dark, where silence speaks,
A star floats, no companion seeks.
Glimmering cold in the endless night,
A beacon lost, embracing light.

Whispers of the cosmos swift,
Lonely path, adrift, adrift.
Brighter than the shadows cast,
A solitary soul so vast.

Eternal dreams in silken glow,
Journey far where none can go.
Silver tears fall from afar,
Yearning close, the lonely star.

Cradled by the empty void,
A light so pure, yet so devoid.
Witness to the ages past,
A timeless sentry, steadfast.

In the darkness, still it burns,
Every wish and dream it yearns.
Lonely starlight, ever bright,
Guiding through the endless night.

Unswerving Luster

Midnight skies hold gleaming fire,
In each glow, a heart's desire.
Unyielding shine, so cool and pure,
A radiance that will endure.

Stoic beams through velvet night,
Guiding wanderers with its light.
Firmly placed in heaven's dome,
Beacon for the lost that roam.

Luminescent, strong and bold,
Endless stories to be told.
Through the epochs, through the time,
Glimmers echo, soft, sublime.

Through the shroud of dreams undreamt,
Hope and strength it still has lent.
Luster bright, unswerving true,
In the darkness, brightly hue.

Eternal sparks our spirits hold,
In each streak, a tale unfolds.
Unswerving luster, never fades,
Through the cosmos, light cascades.

Candles in the Shadows

Flicker gently, whisper slow,
Candles in the shadow's glow.
Guardians of the midnight hours,
In their warmth, the night empowers.

Shadows dance upon the walls,
Silent footsteps softly calls.
Ancient secrets, tales untold,
In the flames, we see unfold.

Winds may blow outside, so fierce,
Yet these lights the dark will pierce.
In their glow, the shadows fade,
Light and dark in ether trade.

Through the night, their vigils keep,
Sacred flames that never sleep.
Hope and warmth they bring anew,
Candlelight and shadows true.

Silent sentinels they stand,
Guiding light with gentle hand.
Candles in the shadows bright,
Guardians of eternal night.

Under the Ebony Sky

Beneath the world of twilight dreams,
The sky of ebony, it seems,
Paints the night with sable folds,
A canvas where the wonder holds.

Stars alight in scattered grace,
Jewels across the darkened space.
Every twinkle, every shine,
Speaks of secrets so divine.

Winds of starlight softly blow,
Whispers in the night they sow.
Underneath the cosmic sea,
Endless depths of mystery.

Cloaked in midnight's soft embrace,
Lost in time and cosmic space.
An endless realm, no bounds to see,
Under the sky, the spirit's free.

Ebony sky, with stars so bright,
Guiding through the mist of night.
Eternal night, our hearts held high,
Wandering under the ebony sky.

Night's Silent Savior

In shadows long and thick they rove,
Whispers carried on the breeze,
Night's embrace in velvet glove,
Draped in moonlight through the trees.

Stars ignite with fervent spark,
Guiding souls through dark and drear,
Silent savior in the dark,
Eclipses every lingering fear.

Oceans hum with gentle waves,
Cradling dreams in tender light,
Hidden depths where courage saves,
Strengthened by the quiet night.

Beneath the endless ebon sky,
Wisdom flows from ancient lore,
Silent saviors hover nigh,
Guarding peace forevermore.

Unyielding Glow

Beneath a shroud of twilight dim,
A beacon lights the darkened way,
Unyielding glow, a timeless hymn,
    That keeps the fears at bay.

Mountains stand with silent pride,
Their peaks kissed by celestial gleams,
Guiding hearts through what betide,
    Awakening forgotten dreams.

Through valleys deep and forests vast,
The glow persists where shadows creep,
A constant light from ages past,
Transcending both the wake and sleep.

Forth the glow in firm resolve,
Breaching bounds of mortal sight,
In its warmth, all doubts dissolve,
Unyielding through the endless night.

Luminous Perseverance

Against the storm and tempest wild,
A light endures, unbent, unbowed,
Like laughter from a distant child,
It pierces every gathering cloud.

Through torrents harsh and despair's gale,
Luminous strength stands ever bright,
Its golden rays will never fail,
A beacon in the heart of night.

With steadfastness it shines anew,
Upon the path of weary souls,
Cooling fears and chasing blue,
Restoring hearts to wholesome wholes.

In shadows deep, through tests severe,
The light endures without a doubt,
Its brilliant gleam forever clear,
Banishing the darkest bout.

Radiance Unseen

Invisible but always there,
A shimmer felt within the heart,
Radiance that fills the air,
Even when the light departs.

Guiding hands unseen, unknown,
Through trials fierce, through nights so long,
With a glow that's softly shown,
In whispers of a tranquil song.

In moments when the shadows fall,
And silence grips the weary mind,
Radiance unseen stands tall,
A comfort in the maze we find.

Beyond the veil of sight and sound,
In spaces where the dreams convene,
There the purest glow is found,
In the realm of radiance unseen.

Stars' Whispered Secrets

In the twilight's tender arms,
A dance of light and shadow forms,
Silent tales of distant charms,
In galaxies where mystery storms.

Whispers thread the evening sky,
Stories of celestial lore,
Ancient secrets drawing nigh,
In constellations to explore.

Through the night, the whispers weave,
Patterns on the moonlit sea,
Every star a verse to leave,
In the vast cosmology.

Planets hum their hidden song,
Odes to distant, unseen suns,
Galaxies where spirits throng,
Where the cosmic journey runs.

In the shadows, light does hide,
Secrets of the universe,
Symphonies of space and tide,
Written in the stars' own verse.

Veiled Luminosity

In shadows deep, the light does play,
A dance of hidden, fleeting gleam,
Mysteries in night's array,
A glow that dreams within a dream.

Moon-kissed mist on midnight's shore,
Silver tendrils softly flow,
Veiled whispers evermore,
In the night, their secrets grow.

Through the blinds of evening's fold,
Glow of phantoms softly tread,
Glimmering tales untold,
Luminescence lightly shed.

Crimson hues and azure light,
Blend their secrets in the dark,
Vestiges of dawn's first sight,
Whispers where the echoes spark.

Through the veils of night they weave,
Glows that hide yet softly show,
Eternal lights that never leave,
Luminous what darkness sows.

A Lantern's Tale

In the grip of twilight's hand,
A lantern's glow begins to rise,
Casting light on shadowed land,
Guiding under darkened skies.

Flickers in the eerie mist,
Weaving dreams where shadows play,
Luminescence warm and kissed,
A beacon in the haunting gray.

A tale of ghosts and ancient lore,
Writ within its gentle flame,
Nights of wonder, long before,
Where each glow recalled a name.

Silent stories, whispers old,
Told by light so soft and kind,
Embers weave the tale they hold,
Written in the glow's confined.

As the night gives way to dawn,
Lantern's tale fades in the light,
Memories by morning drawn,
Woven in the fabric of the night.

Ignite the Pitch

In the heart of blackened night,
Embers spark to life and glow,
Threads of orange through the blight,
A dance where shadows dare not go.

Flame ignites the pitch dark air,
Whispers of a blazing tune,
Light to guide through dark despair,
Illumining both sun and moon.

Phoenix from the shadows rise,
Burning bright with vivid hue,
In the darkness, light defies,
Soul in flame, both fierce and true.

Every ember, fierce and free,
Turns the night to daylight's edge,
Boldly burning, wild decree,
In the fire, we make our pledge.

Let the torch of night be lit,
Casting out the dark so cold,
Through the pitch, the fire-lit,
Forge a tale of light, retold.

The Hidden Shining

In shadows where the whispers creep,
A spark ignites, a secret keep,
Throughout the night, within the deep,
A hidden shining stirs from sleep.

Through silent woods, on moonlit streams,
A glimmer threads through quiet dreams,
In places where the stillness seams,
A hidden shining softly gleams.

Beneath the stars, across the sky,
Unknown to those who pass it by,
An essence that can never lie,
A hidden shining lives, though shy.

In hearts confined by endless night,
A buried flame begins its flight,
Unseen by those who look for light,
A hidden shining burns too bright.

So seek the realms where shadows play,
To find the light that does not stay,
In corners where the dark holds sway,
A hidden shining lights the way.

Unseen Luminance

In darkness where the secrets lie,
A glow that few can testify,
Beyond the reach of mortal eye,
Unseen luminance waits nearby.

Beneath the cover of the night,
A brilliance cloaked from human sight,
Within the depths, a ghostly light,
Unseen luminance shining bright.

In places where the silence speaks,
A hidden radiance softly leaks,
Through cracks and crevices, it seeks,
Unseen luminance never weak.

Though hidden from the common gaze,
Its presence weaves through endless maze,
In muted tones, in twilight's haze,
Unseen luminance lights our days.

So listen to the silent call,
Feel light that shadows do install,
In unseen corners, one and all,
Unseen luminance guards the hall.

Reflective Dark

In blackened glass, the shadows dance,
A mirror to the soul's expanse,
In twilight's grip, a ghostly trance,
Reflective dark takes wild chance.

Across the void where stars reside,
A darkness that will not collide,
In stillness where the echoes hide,
Reflective dark runs deep and wide.

The night is but a canvas bare,
Of whispers caught within the air,
In places where the brave despair,
Reflective dark is always there.

Through corridors of endless night,
A world within devoid of light,
Inhesitant steps, the heart's pure plight,
Reflective dark, our guiding sight.

Beyond the dreams, where fears reside,
A truth that shadows do not bide,
In hidden realms where thoughts confide,
Reflective dark stands by our side.

Through the Veil

Beyond the reach of mortal hand,
A realm where mystic shadows stand,
Within the haze, a foreign land,
Through the veil of time and sand.

In spaces where the light does bend,
Silent whispers, messages send,
In shadows where the worlds transcend,
Through the veil, the minds extend.

A journey through the misty flow,
To places no one else can go,
In depths where ancient rivers know,
Through the veil, the truths bestow.

Unseen by eyes that seek the light,
A realm where day turns into night,
In shrouded whispers, out of sight,
Through the veil, the spirits might.

So wander forth with open heart,
Embrace the shadows, play your part,
In hidden realms where dreams do start,
Through the veil, life's hidden art.

Light

Amidst the dark, a beacon bright,
A guiding torch through endless night,
In heart and soul, a gentle might,
The light that brings the world to sight.

Through shadows cast by doubt and fear,
A radiance that draws us near,
In places where the path unclear,
The light that whispers words sincere.

Beyond the veil of twilight's grip,
A luminescence steady, slip,
In every breath, in every lip,
The light that steers the fate's own ship.

In quiet moments filled with grace,
A glow that none can displace,
In every heart, in every face,
The light that time cannot erase.

So cherish every fleeting gleam,
In darkened hours, let it beam,
For in the night, within the dream,
The light will always reign supreme.

Veins of Gold in Coal

Deep within the earth's dark hold,
Amidst the shadows, coarse and cold,
Lies a secret, proud and bold:
Veins of gold in mines of coal.

Pressure forms where few dare tread,
Glistening secrets, stories spread,
Within the black, pure light is bled,
From veins of gold, unsung, unsaid.

In caverns deep, where fear takes hold,
Hope shines bright in veins of gold,
A beacon strong as tales unfold,
Veins of gold in blackened coal.

Hidden paths and tales untold,
Beneath the weight of ages old,
Seek and find what time has sold,
Precious veins, the silent gold.

In the depths where night is whole,
Lies the dream, both young and old,
Victory in spirit bold,
Veins of gold within the coal.

Charlie's Radiant Path

Across the fields where shadows lay,
Charlie treads at break of day,
With a heart that lights the way,
Guiding steps, come what may.

Through the town and past the glen,
Charlie finds his way again,
Blazing trails through dark and fen,
Leaving marks with his bright pen.

Where the forest meets the dawn,
Charlie's light keeps shining on,
In his path, no hope is gone,
Radiant glow from dusk to dawn.

From the streams to mountains high,
Underneath the endless sky,
Charlie's path is bright and nigh,
Radiant love will never die.

Guiding souls with gentle hand,
Leaving prints upon the sand,
Charlie's path, a glowing strand,
Radiant heart in every land.

Hope Among Shadows

In places where the darkness lies,
A spark of light will surely rise,
Glimmer faint beneath the skies,
Hope among the shadows flies.

In every heart where fear has grown,
A whispering of the unknown,
Hope's soft murmur, gently sown,
Strength to claim what we've outgrown.

Among the trees where shadows play,
A beam of light breaks through the gray,
Guiding lost ones on their way,
Hope's embrace in night and day.

The darkest paths, they cannot bind,
The spirit strong, the wandering mind,
For even here, a light we find,
Hope among shadows, intertwined.

So take a step in faith so pure,
Through shadowed lanes, let hope endure,
A beacon bright, a heart secure,
Hope among shadows will allure.

Faint Candlelight

In the stillness of the night,
Through the dark, a gentle light,
Flickering, yet holding tight,
Guiding souls by candlelight.

In a world where shadows creep,
Where dreams lie dormant, lost asleep,
A faint flame promises to keep,
Its silent vigil, clear and deep.

Amid the storm and pressing cold,
Where stories of the heart unfold,
Candlelight, though shy and bold,
Leads us to the truth untold.

Each small flicker, bright and fair,
Illuminates the dark affair,
With its warmth, dispels despair,
Tender glow beyond compare.

So in the gloom, when fears take flight,
Look to the flame, the shining bright,
Whispering of hope's delight,
In the faintest candlelight.

Light Against the Odds

In shadows deep where fear resides,
A glimmer flickers, slow to rise.
Against the dark, a beacon bold,
A tale of light yet to be told.

Through tempest's rage and storm's grim gust,
It fights with fervor, fights with trust.
Unyielding flame in darkest night,
A warrior born to bring the light.

Hope's fragile, brilliant gleam persists,
Through daunting trials it resists.
A spark to blaze, a fire to start,
A light that warms the coldest heart.

Amidst the gloom where shadows dance,
It finds its strength, its chance, its stance.
In every soul where fear remains,
The light of courage breaks its chains.

For those who dare to look within,
The light against the odds will win.
In every heart where shadows lie,
A dawn awaits, the night to fly.

Bright Veil of Night

The night descends, a velvet cloak,
With whispers soft, the stars evoke.
A canopy of dreams untold,
'Neath galaxies, the night unfolds.

In quiet realms where silence sings,
The moonlight weaves its silver strings.
Each twinkling star a guiding light,
To lead us through the velvet night.

Embrace the darkness, feel its peace,
In shadows find a sweet release.
The night reveals what day conceals,
A world where infinite beauty heals.

The bright veil turns a midnight hue,
A mystery, a silent cue.
To those who seek with open hearts,
The night imparts its ancient arts.

In every shadow, light is cast,
A fleeting moment, slow to last.
Through night's embrace, we find our way,
To greet the promise of the day.

Shining in the Pitch

In darkest void where whispers creep,
A single star begins to peep.
Through endless black, it fights to gleam,
A beacon bright; a golden beam.

Its radiance defies the dark,
A glimmer of hope, a tender spark.
In shadows deep where fears abound,
A light emerges, safe and sound.

The pitch of night cannot suppress
The glow that yearns to convalesce.
Though cloaked in black, it fiercely shines,
A testament to light's designs.

In every heart where darkness dwells,
A light of courage softly swells.
Against the void, it stands its ground,
A silent hymn, a hopeful sound.

To those who walk in shadow's wake,
The light within you cannot break.
For shining in the pitch, we see,
A boundless light that sets us free.

Gloaming Resurgence

At twilight's edge where shadows creep,
The world in gentle silence sleeps.
A dusky glow begins its reign,
To wash away the day's refrain.

In hues of crimson, gold, and blue,
The evening paints a wondrous view.
The sun descends, its journey done,
To bid farewell, a setting sun.

Through night's approach, a promise gleams,
Of dreams to come, of whispered dreams.
The gloaming speaks in tender tones,
Of mysteries that night condones.

From dusk to dark, a shift so slight,
A prelude to the deepening night.
In every heart, a spark renews,
A glow that gentle eve imbues.

As stars emerge, the sky reclaims,
A twinkle bright, a thousand flames.
In gloaming's grace, our spirits rise,
To greet the dawn with eager eyes.

Flickers in the Murk

In shadows deep, where whispers twine,
A spark ignites, a fate aligned.
Through mist and moor, the fire does glide,
A beacon called to heart's inside.

In darkest night, the light will surge,
Through veils of fears, the flames emerge.
Soft whispers tell of brighter day,
Where dreams will dance in soft array.

Endless haze may choke the air,
But hope's soft glimmer finds us there.
In every shadow hiding stark
Lies the promise of a spark.

Courage rise through stormy gale,
And let not fear nor doubt prevail.
With flickers guiding on our way,
The murk shall turn to break of day.

When echoes call from realms unseen,
Remember well where you have been.
The journey whispered through the dark,
Guided by the subtle spark.

Beacon Within

A light that shines from deep inside,
Through storm and strife, it's there to guide.
In moments dark and shadows grim,
The beacon's glow will never dim.

When doubt consumes and fears encase,
Look inward to that hopeful space.
A flame that burns so pure and true,
It lights the path for me and you.

In times of loss or endless night,
The beacon rises, golden bright.
It whispers softly to the soul,
Embracing every part, the whole.

Through trials vast and oceans wide,
This inner glow will be our guide.
It pushes through the thickest veil,
Ensuring that we never fail.

So heed the call of light within,
And let its journey now begin.
With every step and every breath,
We'll rise above the tides of death.

Shining Through Despair

In moments bleak, where shadows cling,
A ray of hope starts shimmering.
From hearts that ache and minds that yearn,
A light emerges, bold and stern.

The dark may press with crushing weight,
Yet in its hold, find something great.
For in despair, a gleam will start,
To pour its warmth into the heart.

Against the tide of endless gloom,
A flower blooms, a sweet perfume.
Its petals spread, a beacon rare,
Shining through the deep despair.

No night so long it cannot break,
No sorrow's grasp it cannot shake.
When all seems lost, and paths unclear,
A light persists to conquer fear.

Hold firm to hope, though dark surrounds,
For strength in light is where it's found.
Together we can pierce the night,
And bring the dawn, a brand-new light.

Illumination of Silence

In quietude, where thoughts reside,
A gentle glow begins to guide.
No need for words or loud decree,
Silence speaks in light's decree.

Reflecting depths of the unknown,
A calmness in the dark is sown.
Through stillness, rays of clarity,
Illuminate what eyes can't see.

When chaos roars and tempests rise,
A whispering hush defies the skies.
In silence, truths are gently shared,
A tender comfort, always there.

This quiet light, so soft and pure,
In darkest night, it will endure.
A guiding star in tranquil grace,
It lights the soul's most sacred place.

Embrace the silence, let it heal,
Its gentle glow, so true and real.
For in the stillness, find the way,
A dawn that breaks with each new day.

Within the Dark

In the shadows where whispers reside,
A silent world begins to confide,
The secrets of both old and new,
Silent breezes that gently pursue.

Stars awaken in the velvet night,
Whispers of dreams take their flight,
Mysteries dance upon the breeze,
In the dark, our souls find ease.

The moon's pale glow caresses all,
As evening's curtain starts to fall,
Silent sighs and calm embrace,
Darkness reveals its tender face.

In the corners, hidden and quaint,
Ghostly whispers, soft and faint,
Stories old and stories told,
Darkness wraps them in its fold.

A world within the silent night,
Unseen forces, out of sight,
Within the dark, a calm prevails,
A sanctuary where heart regales.

Glow

A flicker in the dimmest place,
A spark of hope, a warm embrace,
Through the shadows, softly it creeps,
Lighting the path where silence sleeps.

In moments quiet and serene,
A gentle glow, a peaceful sheen,
It paints the world in hues so mild,
With tender rays, both meek and wild.

A beacon in the darkest hour,
Whispering of a hidden power,
Soft luminescence, pure and bright,
Guiding souls through endless night.

Light that dances, glimmers, gleams,
Echoes softly in our dreams,
A radiant touch, a tender trail,
In the glow, our fears grow pale.

Embrace the glow, the gentle light,
Transform the dark into delight,
In every heart, a spark does grow,
Blooming brightly with a glow.

Night's Subtle Gleam

Under the cloak of the midnight sky,
A subtle gleam catches the eye,
Stars that twinkle, whisper low,
In the quiet night, they softly glow.

Mystic shadows softly sway,
In the night, they gently lay,
Every gleam, a secret keeps,
In the stillness, the world sleeps.

Whispers hum in the cool night air,
Songs of dreams, beyond compare,
Glimmers gentle, soft and fair,
Through the darkness, secrets share.

Candles flicker, shadows play,
In the night's embrace, they stay,
Every gleam a story old,
Both unseen and untold.

In the depths of the night's soft hue,
Gleams of silver, white, and blue,
Night's embrace, a sacred theme,
Revealed in every subtle gleam.

Hushed Embers

Fading light and hushed embers,
Warmth of moments one remembers,
In the hearth, a gentle glow,
Silent stories, soft and slow.

Crackling flames, a whispered tale,
Within these walls, old dreams prevail,
Each ember tells a gentle lore,
Of yesteryears and more.

Silent warmth in tender light,
Guides the heart through every night,
A glow that wraps around the soul,
Lost in memories, we become whole.

Shadows dance upon the wall,
Echoed whispers gently call,
In the hush, the embers burn,
To their gentle light, we turn.

Embrace the warmth, the silent fire,
Find the peace within the pyre,
Hushed embers softly send,
Light and warmth until the end.

Surviving Luminance

In the depth of endless night,
Surviving luminance, pure and bright,
A beacon in the darkest hour,
Whispers of a gentle power.

Through the storms, it finds its way,
To shine anew, to light the day,
Every flicker, a hope regained,
Through the shadows, light sustained.

The night may cloak in darkest veil,
Yet the luminance shall prevail,
Surviving through both storm and calm,
It brings a bright and soothing balm.

In hearts it nests, in souls it thrives,
Through every trial, it survives,
Light so tender, pure and bright,
Guiding through the darkest night.

A spark, a flame, a shining star,
No matter where or how far,
Surviving luminance, ever true,
Always there to see us through.

The Persistent Spark

Within the darkest night's embrace,
A spark ignites, defies the gloom,
Its tenacity, a glowing trace
Of hope within an endless room.

Against the winds, it bravely fights,
No storm can dim its fervent gleam,
It whispers through the silent nights,
Embodying a fervent dream.

Through rain and sleet, it stands its ground,
A sentinel in shadowed lands,
In heart of void, where fears abound,
It perseveres, as fate demands.

The smallest ember holds the might,
To kindle flames that pierce the dark,
In scattered ashes, finds the light,
The world restored by its small spark.

So let us guard this fragile glow,
Each spark a beacon, bright and vast,
Together, through the night we'll go,
Our dreams unbroken, shadows cast.

Shadows' Nemesis

In realms where shadows dance and play,
   A force arises, fierce and bright,
   It chases all the dark away,
  Transforming night into pure light.

With golden swords and shields ablaze,
   It battles through the fog of fear,
   Its courage in the bleakest maze,
   A radiant herald drawing near.

No cavern deep, no crevice cold,
  Can hold against its steadfast grace,
  Its blaze unweaving shadows' fold,
And bringing warmth to every space.

Through every dusk, in twilight's chill,
   It stands as nemesis to shade,
   Its will unbent, untamed, until
   The night itself begins to fade.

Oh, guardian of day and dream,
   For every heart, a guiding flame,
In shadows' war, let your light gleam,
  Eternal, bright, without a name.

Fireflies in Twilight

As evening cloaks the sky in hue,
A dance of light begins so shy,
In twilight's tender, soft debut,
The fireflies awaken, nigh.

They flicker in a whispered code,
A symphony of fleeting sparks,
Across the fields, where dreams erode,
And merge within the canvas dark.

Their glow, a tale of ancient lore,
Of fleeting time and endless space,
Each tiny lantern shining more,
Than all the stars in their embrace.

In silent woods, they weave a spell,
A tapestry of gleaming thread,
Through whispered winds, their secrets tell,
Of life and love and words unsaid.

So let us watch, and let us sigh,
For moments brief, yet brilliant too,
As fireflies in twilight fly,
And paint the night in shades anew.

Gleams Through Obscurity

Within the depths of shadowed veil,
A glimmer threads its ghostly way,
It winds through night, a secret trail,
That leads us to the break of day.

A whisper of the hidden light,
In labyrinths of doubt and fear,
It guides the lost through endless night,
And brings the distant future near.

Through mists of time and pools of haze,
Its gleams illuminate the past,
Revealing truths in subtle ways,
A beacon shining strong and vast.

So follow not the darkest bend,
But seek the glimmers bright and true,
For hope and light, they never end,
Their paths are there for me and you.

In every soul, a spark resides,
To pierce the thickest obscurity,
Embrace the light, let go of tides,
And see the world with clarity.

Printed in the USA
CPSIA information can be obtained
at www.ICGtesting.com
CBHW071816180724
11673CB00023B/756